ALL ABOUT ME

My Birth

CARYN JENNER

W
FRANKLIN WATTS
LONDON · SYDNEY

First published in 2014

Franklin Watts
338 Euston Road
London NW1 3BH

Franklin Watts Australia
Level 17/207 Kent Street
Sydney, NSW 2000

Series editor: Sarah Peutrill
Art director: Jonathan Hair
Design: www.rawshock.co.uk
Consultant: Mr Robert Holmes, FRCOG

Dewey number: 306.8'5
ISBN: 978 1 4451 2973 0
Printed in China

Franklin Watts is a division of
Hachette Children's Books,
an Hachette UK company.
www.hachette.co.uk

CONTENTS

(Words in **bold** are in the glossary on page 28.)

THE BEGINNING OF YOU

Have you ever wondered how you were made? You know that you used to be a baby. You might also know that you grew inside your mum's tummy. But how did you become a baby, and how were you born? To find out, let's go back to the very beginning of you.

This is Felix. He is eight years old.

A MUM AND A DAD

Everyone is made by a mum and a dad. The mum has special **eggs** inside her body. The dad also has special things in his body, called **sperm**. A baby begins to grow when one of the dad's sperm joins with one of the mum's eggs.

This is Felix when he was a baby, with his mum and dad. He began when one of his dad's sperm joined with his mum's egg.

The parents who made you – your birth parents – may not be the only mum and dad you have. For example, you may also have a step-mum or step-dad who is married to one of your birth parents, or you may have been adopted.

IN MUM'S TUMMY

The baby starts in the mum's tummy as one tiny **cell**, a single building block from which the rest of the baby grows. Gradually, the baby develops arms and legs, and eyes and ears, and everything needed to become a little person. After about nine months in the mum's tummy, the baby is ready to be born.

Before Felix was born, he grew in his mum's tummy for about nine months.

BABY-MAKING SYSTEMS

The parts of the body that are used for making babies are called the reproductive system. Women and men have different reproductive systems. Between the ages of about 11 and 15, you will go through a stage of life called puberty, when your reproductive system will get ready to make babies.

A WOMAN'S SYSTEM

Inside her body, a woman has two **ovaries**, where her eggs are stored. Each egg is about the size of this full stop. Every month, an egg leaves one of her ovaries and passes through a **tube** to her **womb**. At the bottom of the womb is the **cervix**, which leads to a kind of tunnel called the **vagina**, or birth canal.

The mum's egg travels from her ovary through a tube to her womb.

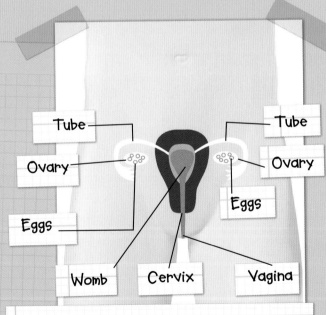

Tube Ovary Eggs Tube Ovary Eggs Womb Cervix Vagina

This diagram shows the female reproductive system.

If the woman's egg does not join with a man's sperm, the egg will come out through her vagina, along with blood from the lining of her womb. This is known as a woman's monthly period.

A MAN'S SYSTEM

A man has two **testicles**, also called balls. These are protected by a bag of skin called the **scrotum** which hangs outside his body. During puberty, a man's body starts making millions and millions of sperm in his testicles. The sperm look like tiny tadpoles, with tails that help them to swim. The sperm come out of the man's **penis** or willy.

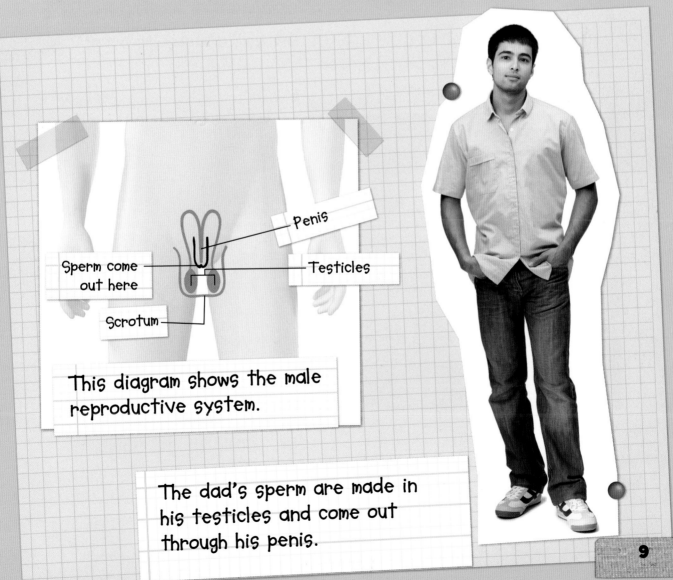

Penis

Sperm come out here

Testicles

Scrotum

This diagram shows the male reproductive system.

The dad's sperm are made in his testicles and come out through his penis.

How does the sperm get to the egg? It starts when a man and woman have a kind of grown-up cuddle.

THE SPERM SETS OFF

This cuddle is known as making love, or having **sex**. The man's penis fits into the woman's vagina. Millions of tiny sperm come out of the man's penis and into the woman's vagina. They swim up through her vagina, her cervix and her womb to her tubes, where the sperm may find an egg.

These are three drawings of the egg and sperm race, which are shown much bigger than in real life.

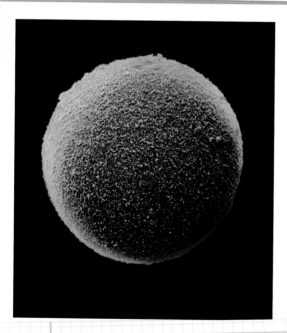

One egg is released from the mum's ovary into her tubes.

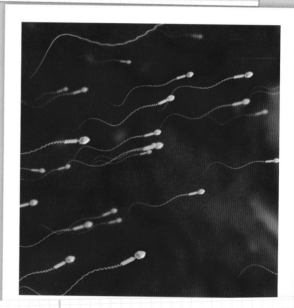

Millions of the dad's sperm race towards the egg.

THE SPERM'S JOURNEY

The sperm are so tiny that hundreds of them could fit onto the head of a pin. Some sperm are stronger and faster than others. Only a few hundred sperm out of the millions that come out of the man's penis reach the tubes.

Making love is a way for grown-ups to show that they love each other. But if they don't want to make a baby, they use birth control, called a contraceptive, to stop the sperm and egg from joining.

THE EGG AND SPERM MEET

The first sperm to reach the egg is the winner. The moment one of your dad's sperm joined with your mum's egg was the beginning of you. The joining of the sperm and the egg is called **fertilisation**. As soon as a sperm fertilises the egg, a special coating forms which stops other sperm from joining with the egg too.

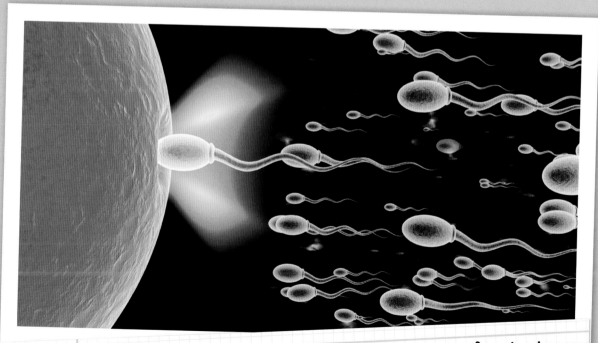

The winning sperm joins with the egg. This is the first step in making a baby.

ONE OF A KIND

The egg and sperm contain genes, which are special instructions that combine to make you who you are. For instance, your genes decide the colour of your skin, hair and eyes, as well as how tall you could be when you grow up.

GIRL OR BOY?

The genes in the father's sperm decide whether a baby will be a girl or a boy. All of the mum's eggs have X genes. Some of the dad's sperm have X and some have Y. If an egg is fertilised by an X-sperm, it makes an XX combination and the baby will be a girl. But if an egg is fertilised by a Y-sperm, it makes an XY combination and the baby will be a boy.

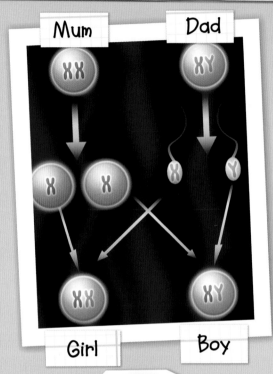

Mum   Dad

Girl   Boy

An XX combination of genes makes a girl, while an XY combination makes a boy.

12

TWINS

Sometimes, the mum's ovaries release two eggs which are fertilised by two different sperm. The result is two babies - twins who share the mum's womb.

IDENTICAL TWINS

Identical twins happen when one fertilised egg divides to become two separate babies. Identical twins look alike because they share the same genes from exactly the same egg and sperm. But identical twins are never exactly the same - each is still one of a kind.

Louisa and Sophie look almost exactly alike because they are identical twins.

People in the same family often look similar because they share some of the same genes. Can you see how Troy and his family look similar?

Once the sperm fertilises the egg, the egg has a lot of growing and changing to do in order to become a baby. Imagine - by the time you were born, you were about 10 billion times bigger than the original egg cell.

A BALL OF CELLS

The egg starts growing in the mum's tube. It divides into two cells, those cells divide to make four cells, then eight cells, and so on. Each time, the number of cells doubles. While it is growing the egg moves from the tube into the womb. By the time it reaches the womb, about a week after fertilisation, it has grown to be a ball of up to a hundred cells and it is now called an **embryo**.

By the time the egg reaches the womb, it has grown into a ball of over a hundred cells.

All living things are made of tiny building blocks called cells.
Each type of cell has a different job. For example, your bones are made up of different sorts of cells from your muscles. Can you think of other types of cells in your body?

A TINY BEING

The ball of cells grows longer. Some cells become the baby's heart, which begins to beat. Other cells form bumps on the body. These bumps grow into arms and legs. The brain starts to develop and the face begins to appear, with dark spots for eyes and tiny slits on the side for ears. After about six weeks, it is called a **fetus**. It stays in the mother's womb for nine months, when it is born.

Occasionally, a fetus dies before it can be born. This is called a miscarriage.

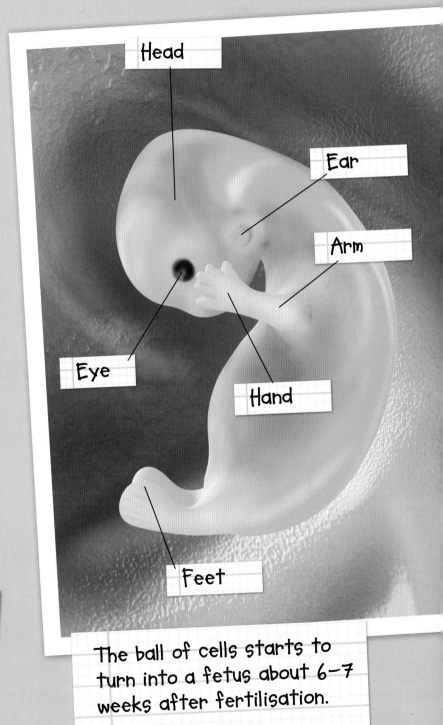

Head

Ear

Arm

Eye

Hand

Feet

The ball of cells starts to turn into a fetus about 6–7 weeks after fertilisation.

After about two months in your mum's body, you were already looking like a tiny baby - about the size of a jelly bean. Compared to your body, your head was very large. That's because your brain was growing so quickly.

IN THE WOMB

As the fetus's brain develops, **organs** in the body - such as the lungs, liver and kidneys - begin developing too. These organs will help the baby to survive once it is born. After about three months in the mum's womb, the fetus can open and close its mouth. But at this stage of development, its eyes stay shut, even when it is awake.

A pregnant mum might feel a little sick at first, as her body gets used to having a growing baby in her womb.

As Maria's baby grew in her womb, so did the bump in her tummy.

MOVING ABOUT

The baby develops a bony skeleton. Its muscles are developing too, and it moves about in the mum's womb. It starts with small movements, such as turning its head, moving its fingers and toes, and sucking its thumb. By about the fifth month, the baby is so lively that the mum can feel it kicking, rolling around - and even hiccuping.

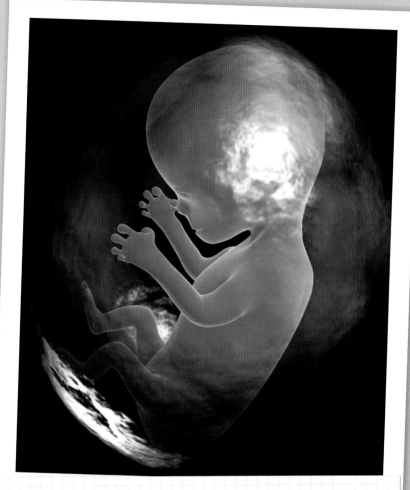

This baby has been growing in its mum's body for three months.

INSIDE THE WOMB

Inside your mum's womb, it was cosy and warm. It was just the right temperature to keep you comfortable as you floated inside a soft, squishy cushion of liquid called amniotic fluid.

AMNIOTIC SAC

The amniotic fluid is inside a bag called the **amniotic sac**. This surrounds the baby and keeps it safe. Inside the amniotic sac, the baby can hear the soothing thump-thump of its mum's heartbeat. The baby can hear her voice too, and other sounds outside the mum's womb.

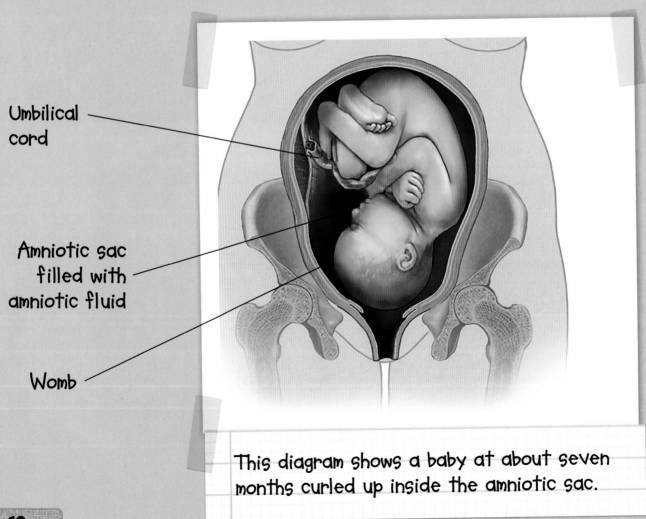

Umbilical cord

Amniotic sac filled with amniotic fluid

Womb

This diagram shows a baby at about seven months curled up inside the amniotic sac.

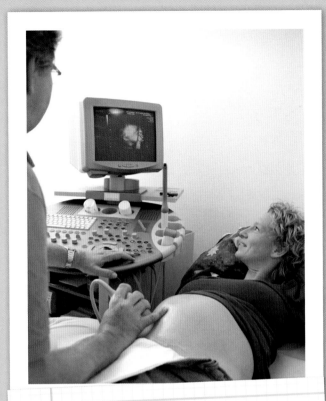

The doctor uses an ultrasound scanner to see the baby in Tilly's womb.

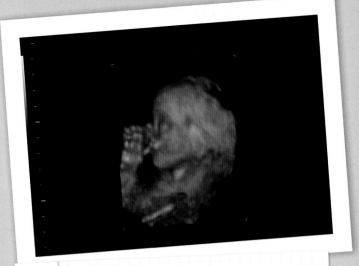

This 3-D ultrasound picture shows Tilly's baby sucking its thumb in her womb.

UMBILICAL CORD

The baby can't eat or breathe until it is born, so it survives by getting oxygen and **nutrients** from the mum's blood. A tube called the **umbilical cord** carries the mum's blood to the baby inside the womb. If the mum has a healthy diet while she's pregnant, the baby in her tummy will have a healthy diet too.

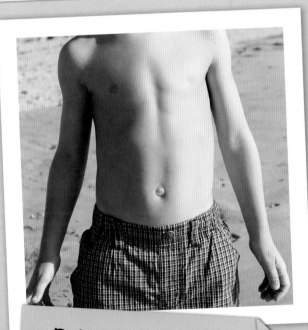

? Did you ever wonder why you have a belly button? This is where your umbilical cord was attached.

ALMOST READY...

After a while, your mum's tummy probably started to look like a big beach ball! Inside her womb, you were still growing and changing until - after about nine months - you were a complete little human being, ready to be born.

GROWING BIGGER

During the last few months of pregnancy, the baby grows quickly, putting on a layer of fat that will keep it warm and help it survive outside the womb. After seven months in the womb, a baby usually weighs about 1.5 kg, the same as a small bag of sugar. But by the time the baby is born, it will weigh three or four times more than that.

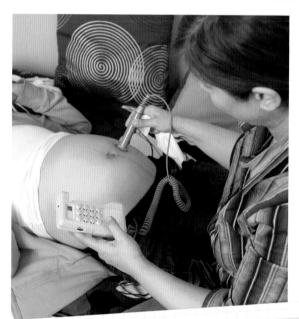

Rachel's midwife (see page 22) listens to the baby's heartbeat with a mini scanner. She is nine months pregnant, so the baby should come soon.

THE FINAL DETAILS

After about nine months, the baby is fully formed. Its lungs are ready to breathe in air as soon as it is born. It can open and close its eyes, and see light coming through the womb. It even has tiny nails on its fingers and toes, and hair on its head. The baby turns around in the womb so that its head is pointing downwards, ready to enter the world.

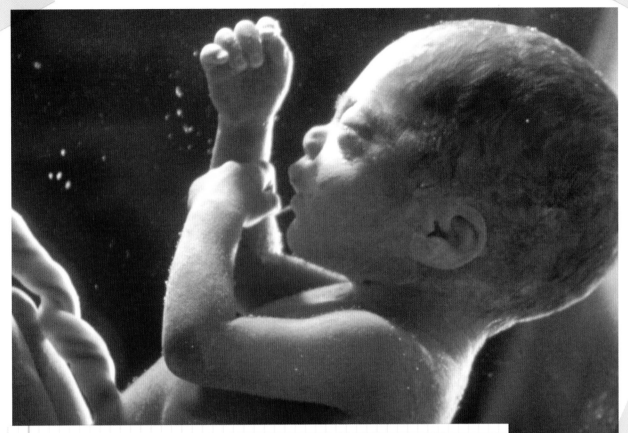

This baby is fully grown and ready to be born!

The parents will need lots of things for the new baby, such as a cot for the baby to sleep in. What other things will they need?

Mara uses a doll to show a couple how to bath a baby.

BEING BORN

Inside your mum's womb, you spent nine months growing from a tiny egg into a baby. When you were finally ready to be born, you squeezed your way out of her womb and into the world.

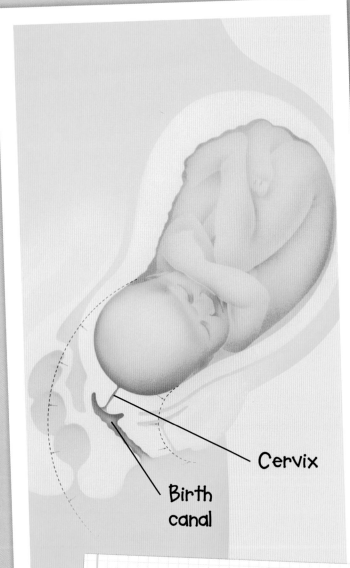

Cervix

Birth canal

Slowly, the cervix opens to let the baby squeeze out of the mother's womb and into the birth canal.

LABOUR

Giving birth is often called **'labour'** because it is hard work and very tiring for both the mum and the baby. It can take many hours. The mother gets a tight feeling in her womb called a **contraction** that comes and goes. The contractions gradually get stronger and come more often. As the baby begins coming out of the womb, the amniotic sac breaks open and the fluid comes out.

A midwife is specially trained to look after women during pregnancy and childbirth.

HERE COMES BABY

The mum uses all her strength to push the baby through the birth canal. It is like a narrow tunnel that widens just enough to let the baby squeeze through. At last, the baby's big head comes out first, followed by the rest of the body.

Sometimes, doctors deliver the baby directly from the womb by an operation called a Caesarean section.

'Waaahhh!' Liv's first cry as she is born is a good sign that she is breathing.

You can't remember your first moments of life after you were born. But after nine months in your mum's safe, cosy womb, the bright, busy world outside might have seemed quite confusing.

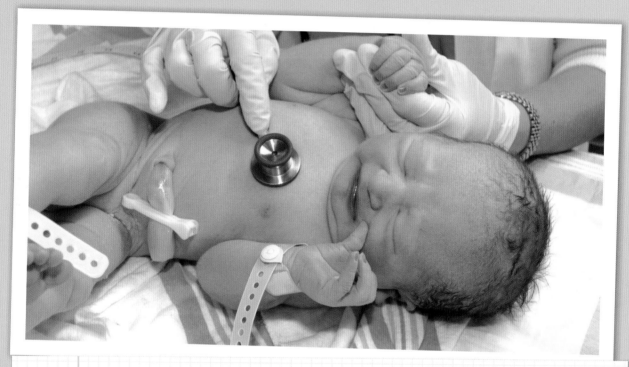

The doctor uses a stethoscope to listen to Ava's heartbeat. The clip shows where the umbilical cord has been cut.

CHECKING THE BABY

Once the baby is born, the umbilical cord is cut. The baby doesn't need this lifeline to its mother in the outside world.

A doctor or midwife gently cleans the amniotic fluid from the baby, then weighs and measures it. They check the baby's heartbeat and make sure that it is healthy.

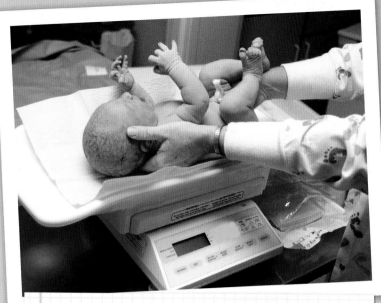

Veronica weighs 3.5 kg, which is about average for a newborn baby.

BABY SKILLS

A newborn baby may already recognise its mum's voice and smell from being in the womb. It knows how to suck so it is able to feed, usually on milk from its mother's breast. A newborn baby waves its arms and legs about because it can't yet control its movements. But as the baby grows bigger and stronger, it will learn many new skills, such as smiling and sitting up.

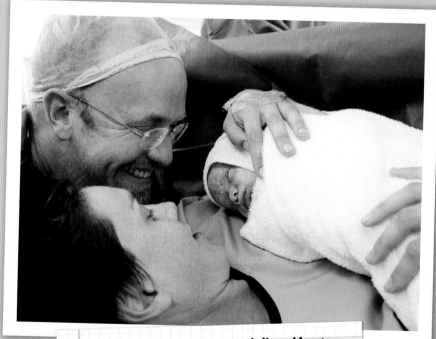

Polly and Andy cuddle their newborn baby. They're still deciding what to name her.

Newborn babies can see close-up, but they must learn to focus on far away things.

LOOKING AFTER BABY

Having a baby also means looking after it once it's born - and that's hard work! The baby needs its mum and dad to do everything for it. When you were a newborn baby, you needed constant care and attention, and lots of love.

A BABY NEEDS CARE

Babies can't do many of the things that bigger people can do. They can sleep, feed, burp, wee, poo - and cry a lot. If the baby is hungry, cold, has a wet nappy, or just wants a cuddle, it cries to let people know. With help, a baby is very good at growing and learning, but it can't look after itself.

Baby Adela breastfeeds on her mother's milk.

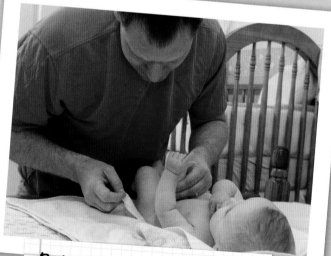

Baby Morgan's dad changes his wet nappy.

Baby Joe gets lots of kisses from his mum.

Jaydon helps to look after his baby brother.

JUST THE START...

Imagine, you began as a dot smaller than a full stop. Then, during the nine months that you were in your mum's tummy, you grew and grew and grew. It was the biggest growth spurt of your life. And then you were born. That was just the start of a whole life ahead for a unique human being - you!

Amniotic fluid liquid in the amniotic sac that protects a baby in the womb

Amniotic sac the bag in the mother's womb that surrounds the baby as it grows

Caesarean section surgery to deliver a baby directly from the mother's womb

Cell a tiny unit that together with other cells makes up a living thing

Cervix the opening between a woman's womb and vagina

Contraceptive a way of stopping the sperm and egg from making a baby

Contraction tight feeling in a woman's womb when she is in labour during birth

Egg a human egg is a tiny cell stored in a woman's ovary. When it is fertilised by sperm from a man, it can grow into a baby

Embryo the name for the developing baby from about two to eight weeks

Fertilisation when a man's sperm joins with a woman's egg

Fetus the name for the developing baby from about six weeks until it is born

Genes the instructions inside human cells that decide whether a baby is a girl or a boy, and many other things like their height and hair colour

Labour when a mother is in the process of giving birth to a baby, it is said that she is 'in labour'

Midwife someone trained to help women during pregnancy and childbirth

Nutrients food needed to survive and grow

Organs parts of the body that do certain jobs, such as the heart pumping blood or the lungs breathing

Ovaries a woman has two ovaries in her body where her eggs are stored. Every month one of her ovaries releases an egg

Penis also called a 'willy'. Sperm comes out of a man's penis

Pregnant a woman is pregnant when she has a baby growing in her womb

Puberty a stage of the life cycle in which a person begins to grow into an adult

Reproductive system the parts of the body that make it possible to have a baby

Scrotum a wrinkly bag of skin that holds the man's testicles

Sex a cuddle between grown-ups when sperm comes out of a man's penis into a woman's vagina. Having sex is the first step to making a baby

Sperm the male sex cell that is released during sex and joins with an egg inside the female body to make a baby

Stethoscope a medical tool used to listen to the heartbeat and breathing

Testicles also called 'balls', testicles are where a man's body makes millions of sperm

Tubes a woman's egg travels from one of her ovaries through a tube to her womb. The full name is the fallopian tubes

Ultrasound scanner a machine that uses sound waves to get a picture of the inside of the body

Umbilical cord tube that brings oxygen and nutrients from the mother's blood to the baby

Vagina opening in a woman's body, also known as the birth canal because the baby comes from the womb through the vagina to be born

Womb where the baby grows inside the woman's body until it is born. Also called a uterus

Further information

For adults
Speakeasy: Talking with your children about growing up (Family Planning Association)

Books for children
How Did I Begin? Mick Manning and Brita Granstrom (Franklin Watts)

What Happens When You Are Born and Grow? Jacqui Bailey (Wayland)

INDEX